Alphabet Tales

D0491451

Published by Letterland International Ltd.,
Barton, Cambridge, CB23 7AY, UK

www.letterland.com

Tel: +44 (0)1223 262675
Fax: +44 (0)1223 264126
Email: info@letterland.com

© Letterland International Ltd 2005. All rights reserved.
10 9 8 7 6 5 4 3

ISBN: 978-1-86209-354-6
Product Code: T64

First published 2005. This edition published 2008, 2010.
Letterland ® is a registered trademark of Lyn Wendon.

This material previously appeared in Fun to Learn™ Letterland
published by The Redan Company Ltd.

All rights reserved. No part of this publication may be reproduced, stored in a retrieval system, or
transmitted in any form or by any means, electronic, mechanical, photocopying, recording or
otherwise, without either the prior permission of the Publisher or a licence permitting restricted
copying in the United Kingdom issued by the Copyright Licensing Agency Ltd, 90 Tottenham Court
Road, London W1T 4LP. This book is sold subject to the condition that it shall not by way of trade
or otherwise be lent, hired out or otherwise circulated without the Publisher's prior consent.

British Library Cataloguing in Publication Data
A catalogue record for this publication is available from the British Library

Printed in Singapore

Contents

Annie Apple

Bouncy Ben

Clever Cat

Dippy Duck

Eddy Elephant

Zig Zag Zebra

**Yellow
Yo-yo Man**

Fix-it Max

About this Book

Many thousands of children have learned to read with Letterland, the unique phonics-based teaching system that brings the alphabet vividly to life. Introducing each of the Letterland characters in alphabetical order, *Letterland Alphabet Tales* will both delight young children and help them to develop valuable reading skills.

Generously illustrated, the twenty-three lively stories are specially designed to build children's confidence as they identify the different Letterland characters and read the simple sentences.

Here are just some of the ways you can share this book to help children on the road to reading:

- For children not yet confident about reading independently, read the stories together. Have fun doing funny voices and emphasising the different letter sounds. Draw attention to the link between the sounds and correct letter shapes.

- Look out for the alliteration in each story. For example,

Walter Walrus

Vicky Violet

Uppy Umbrella

**Talking
Tess**

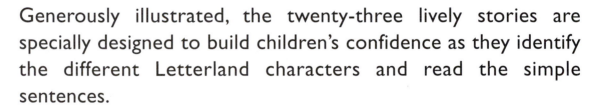

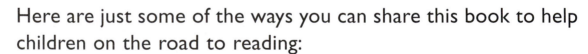

Sammy Snake

Firefighter Fred

Golden Girl

Harry Hat Man

Impy Ink

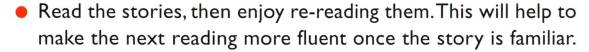
Jumping Jim

Kicking King

Munching Mike's Monster Mask contains words like "mouth", "mirror" and "mum". Play a game asking questions such as, "What might Munching Mike have for breakfast?" "Melon and marmalade?" If the answers are words beginning with Munching Mike's '**mmm**' sound they are bound to be right!

- Always remember to use a letter's sound rather than its name. The Letterland trick to help children remember the correct sound is: START to say a character's name then STOP! The correct sound will be on the child's lips!*

- Read the stories, then enjoy re-reading them. This will help to make the next reading more fluent once the story is familiar.

Lucy Lamp Light

- Use the question at the end of each story to encourage children to look closely at the pictures and talk about what they see. You'll find more questions on page 77.

- Encourage children to trace the Letterlanders' letter shapes with their fingers.

Above all, have fun and enjoy the book together!

*The exception to this rule is **x**, where the correct sound is at the *end* of the character name: Ma**x**.

Munching Mike

Red Robot

Quarrelsome Queen

Peter Puppy

Oscar Orange

Noisy Nick

Annie Apple's rescue act

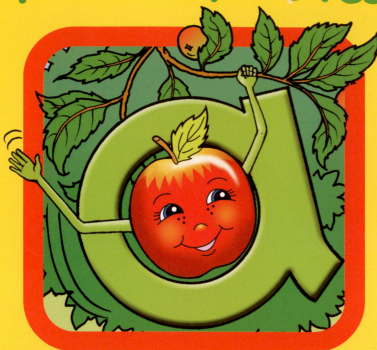

1 Annie Apple is swinging in her tree.

2 She looks across to the farmer's house.

3 Annie spots something at the attic window.

4 "Is that an animal up there?" she asks.

5 Annie tells Firefighter Fred what she's seen.

6 Fred gets his ladder and climbs up to the attic.

7 Look, he's found one of Kicking King's kittens on the window sill. How did she get up there?

8 Just as well Annie Apple spotted her or she'd be there still! Can you see how the kitten climbed up to the attic?

10

Bouncy Ben's big surprise

1 Bouncy Ben bounces out of bed.

2 He eats his breakfast very fast.

3 He's too busy to play ball with his brothers.

4 He's even too busy to go out in his boat.

5 Instead, he picks a bunch of buttercups.

6 Then he blows up a big balloon.

7 Where do you think Ben is going with the balloon and the bunch of buttercups?

8 He's going to see his mum on her birthday! "Happy Birthday, Mum" he says. What have Ben's brother's brought for their mum?

Clever Cat gets cross

Clever Cat is counting things she needs to buy.

1 She needs one pot of cream…

2 …two cup cakes…

3 …three tasty carrots…

4 …four bags of crisps…

5 …and five cool green cucumbers.

6 Clever Cat puts on her coat and drives to the corner shop in her lovely red car.

7 But when she gets there, the shop is shut! "Oh, bother!" says Clever Cat crossly. Can you find the things she needs to buy?

Dippy Duck's drawing game

1 "Let's play a game," says Dippy Duck.

2 "I'll draw something and you guess what it is."

3 "Is it a dish?" asks Clever Cat.

4 "No, it's a drum," says Dippy Duck. "Try again!"

5 "Is it a dog?" asks Clever Cat.

6 "I know!" cries Clever Cat. "It's a donkey!"

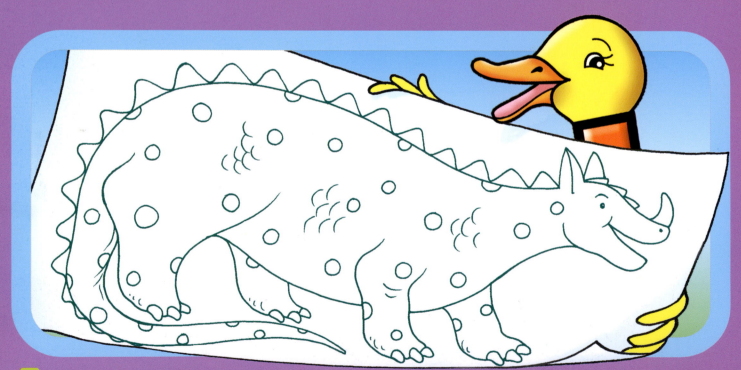

7 "Wrong!" laughs Dippy Duck. "It's a great big dinosaur! Now let's colour it in."

8 Just look at all Dippy Duck's drawings.
Do you know what they are? Which ones begin
with Dippy Duck's sound?

Eddy Elephant's excellent race

1 **What is Eddy Elephant doing?**

2 **Is he going to eat that egg?**

3 **Or is he just going to play with it?**

4 **That spoon looks much too big!**

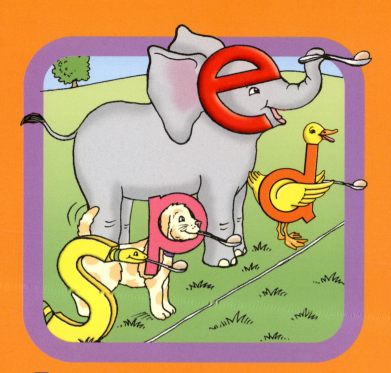

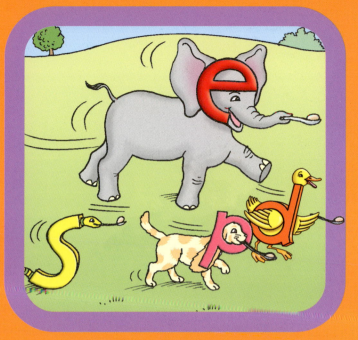

5 Oh, that's what he's doing.

6 It's an egg and spoon race.

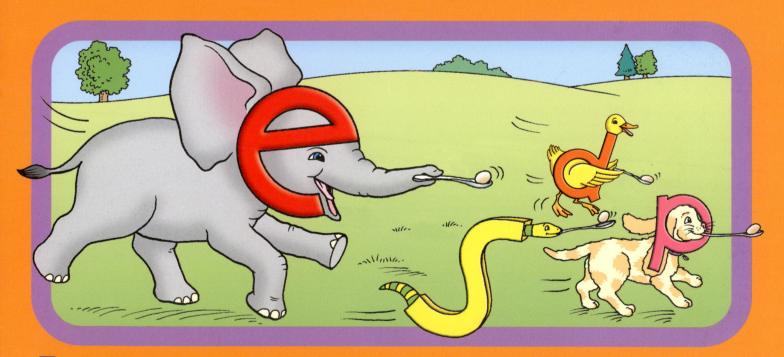

7 He'll have to run faster than that if he's going to win. Run, Eddy, run!

8 Hurray! Eddy Elephant has won the egg and spoon race. Which unlucky Letterlanders have dropped their eggs?

Firefighter Fred on the farm

1 Firefighter Fred is off to help on the farm.

2 First he feeds four fat pigs.

3 Next he fetches some hay on a fork.

4 He fills two buckets with fresh water.

5 And picks some fruit for the farmer.

6 Finally, he finds five speckled eggs.

7 "Thank you all for your help," says the farmer. "Now, would you like to come fishing with me?"

8 Firefighter Fred likes fishing best of all!
How many fish can you see? Can you find four
frogs as well?

Golden Girl's great game

1 Golden Girl is playing with her friends.

2 "Let's play hide and seek," she says.

3 She finds Bouncy Ben behind her gate.

4 She sees Firefighter Fred through the fence.

5 Harry Hat Man is hiding in a heap of hay.

6 But where is Red Robot hiding?

7 "Look!" says Golden Girl with a grin. "Red Robot is running away from my geese!"

8 Who else is hiding in Golden Girl's garden? Someone is hiding in the greenhouse. And who's that behind the tree?

Harry Hat Man's many hats

1 Harry Hat Man makes all kinds of hats.

2 He makes huge hats…

3 …and hard hats…

4 …and Firefighter Fred's helmet.

5 He makes hats for happy children.

6 He even made a hat for his horse Henry.

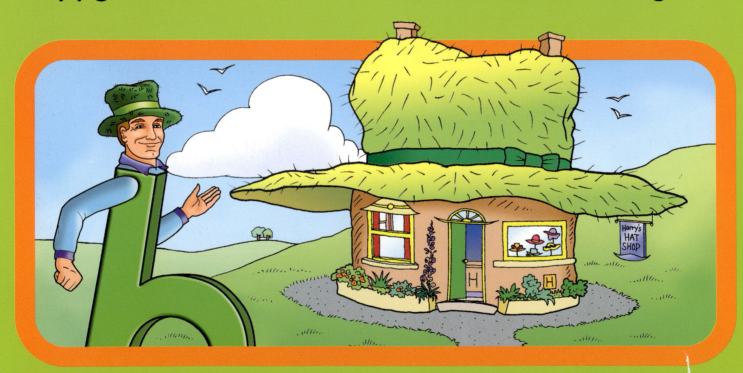

7 And now Harry Hat Man has made a hat for his house!

8 Just look at all the hats Harry Hat Man has made. Can you find a hat for a lady, a cowboy and a wizard? And a hedgehog hiding?

Impy Ink's incredible insects

1 Impy Ink is sitting at his teacher's desk.

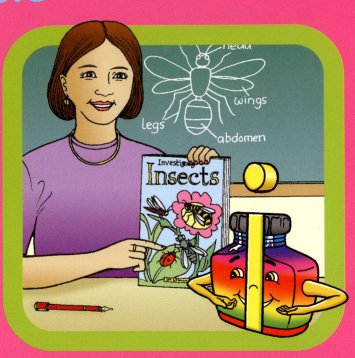

2 His teacher shows him a book about insects.

3 "This butterfly is very pretty indeed."

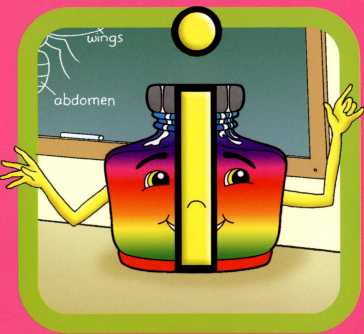

4 Then Impy has an interesting idea.

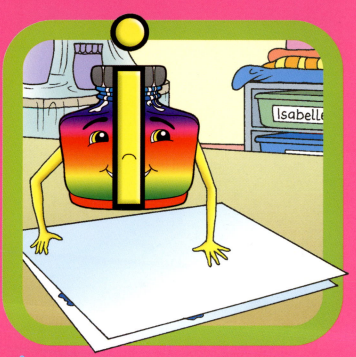

5 Impy pours ink on to some paper. Splat!

6 Then he folds the paper in half.

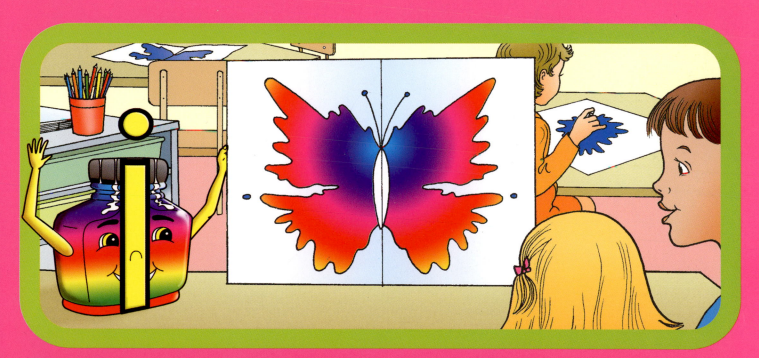

7 When the paper is unfolded, the ink has made an incredible butterfly shape.

8 Look at all the beautiful butterfly pictures.
How many blue butterflies can you count?
Can you see a real butterfly anywhere?

34

Jumping Jim's jolly day

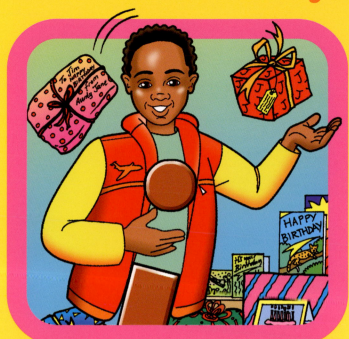

1 It's Jumping Jim's Birthday today.

2 He feels so jolly that he jumps right over...

3 ...his jigsaw puzzle...

4 ...some jam tarts...

35

5 …a jersey from Auntie Jane…

6 …and a jacket from Uncle John.

7 Then Jumping Jim gets so excited he jumps right into the middle of…

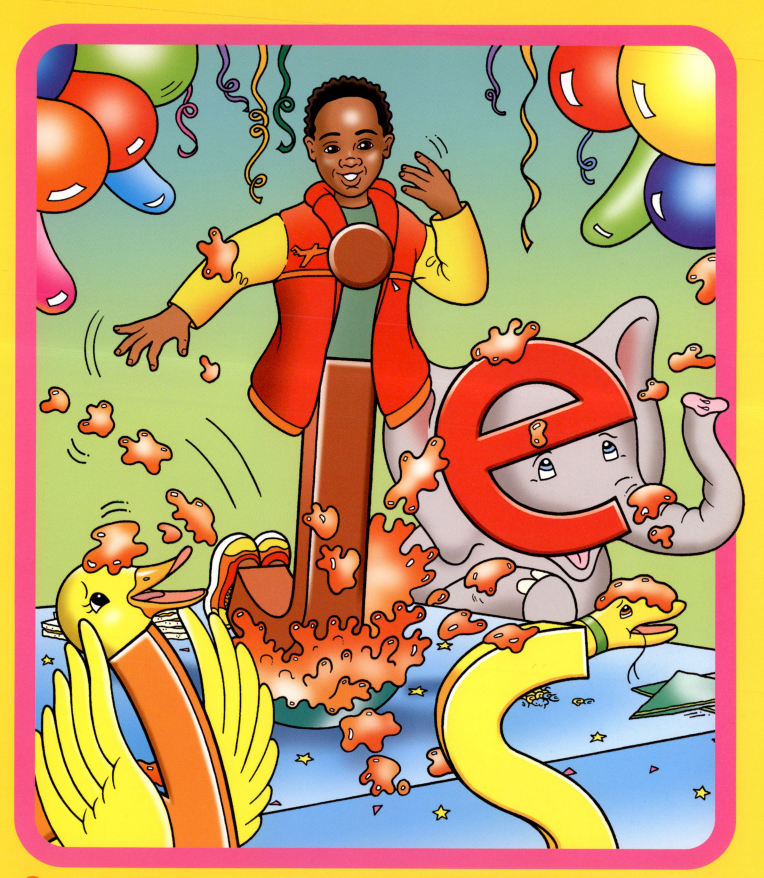

8 ...a big bowl of jelly! Splosh! Who has Jumping Jim splashed jelly all over?

Kicking King's kittens

1 Kicking King is going to fly his kite.

2 "My kite is very plain," he says.

3 "I know! I'll paint a kangaroo on it."

4 So Kicking King gets out his paints.

5 Then he goes to put the kettle on.

6 He doesn't see what his kittens are up to.

7 "My kite isn't plain anymore!" laughs Kicking King when he sees what the kittens have done.

8 Can you find Kicking King's kite? Who do all the other kites belong to? Follow the strings and find out.

40

Lucy Lamp Light lights the way

1 Lucy Lamp Light lives in a lighthouse.

2 She can see a long, long way.

3 Lucy can see some large blue lakes.

4 She can see little lambs leaping.

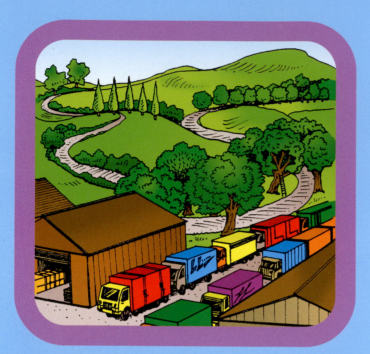

5 She can see lines of lorries and leafy lanes.

6 Lucy can see lots of different things.

7 And at night, everyone else can see her! Look! There's Lucy Lamp Light in her lighthouse!

8 Thank you, Lucy, for shining your light and helping ships find their way. How many ships can you see? Can you count the stars in the night sky?

Munching Mike's monster mask

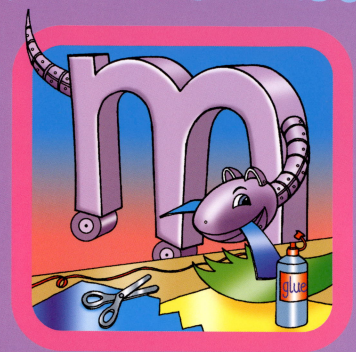

1 Munching Mike is making a mask.

2 First he makes a big wide mouth.

3 Then he makes two big round ears.

4 Next he makes two eyes and a nose.

5 Mike puts the mask on and looks in the mirror.

6 Suddenly, a great big monster appears.

7 But it's only Munching Mike's mum. "It's time to go to the party", she says.

8 All his Letterland friends are there. "This party is mmmarvellous!" says Mike merrily. Can you spot who is behind each mask?

Noisy Nick and the noisy fly

1 Noisy Nick decides to read the newspaper.

2 "I'll be nice and quiet now," he says.

3 Bzzz… "What's that noise?" wonders Nick.

4 A noisy fly has buzzed into the room.

5 The fly buzzes nearer and nearer...

6 ...and lands on Noisy Nick's nose!

7 Noisy Nick takes a swipe at the fly with his newspaper and almost falls out of his chair.

8 Where's that noisy fly gone? Can you see him?
Now see if you can find nine nails hidden in the picture.

Oscar Orange at the docks

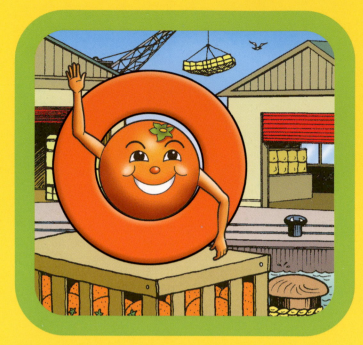

1 Oscar Orange lives down at the docks.

2 The boss is out of the office today.

3 Oscar decides to do the boss's job.

4 There's plenty to do but the office is hot.

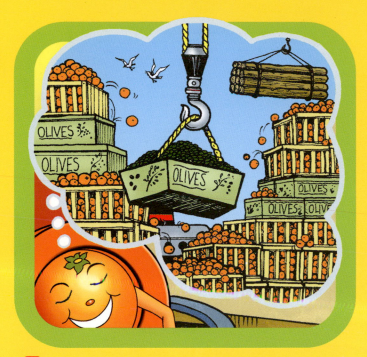 

5 Lots of oranges and olives are unloaded.

6 But a crane drops a load of logs on top!

7 "Stop!" shouts Oscar, waking up with a start. Then he looks outside…

8 …and sees that everything is OK. It had all been a bad dream. How many boxes can you count piled up on the dock?

Peter Puppy pricks his paw

1 Peter Puppy is playing in the park.

2 He pricks his paw on a sharp thorn.

3 "Ouch!" Poor Peter cries with pain.

4 But Clever Cat pulls the thorn out.

5 "You're a brave puppy," she says.

6 She puts a plaster on Peter Puppy's paw.

7 Luckily, Peter Puppy can still play the piano with one paw. He's so proud of his plaster...

8 ...that he asks his friends to come over to show
it off. How many Letterlanders are listening to
Peter Puppy playing the piano?

Quarrelsome Queen and the

1 Look, the Queen is quarreling with a squirrel.

2 "I'm hungry," says the squirrel.

3 "But it's too early to eat!" says the Queen.

4 Quickly, the squirrel runs away.

hungry squirrel

5 He runs up the curtain…

6 …and under the Queen's quilt.

7 Then the squirrel runs along Quarrelsome Queen's umbrella.

8 Now what's he doing? He's quietly nibbling a quarter of the Queen's cake. Can you see how he got to the cake?

Red Robot and the raft

1 Red Robot is running along the road.

2 Suddenly he sees a raft in the river.

3 "I'll take that raft," says Red Robot.

4 He rides on the raft to a rock in the river…

5 …and ties the rope to the rock. But it snaps!

6 Red Robot can't swim so now he's stuck.

7 "I wish I'd never taken that raft," says Red Robot." I hope somebody will rescue me!"

8 Luckily, there are plenty of other Letterlanders close by. Who do you think will rescue him?

Sammy Snake's star gazing

1 Sammy Snake goes to see Talking Tess.

2 "Look into my telescope," says Tess.

3 Sammy Snake looks at the stars in the sky.

4 "I can see something!" he says.

5 "I think that's a satellite," says Tess.

6 "Satellites send signals around the world."

7 "Look, Tess. I can see something else," says Sammy Snake. "Whatever can it be?"

8 "It's a spaceship," says Talking Tess. "And lots of lovely shooting stars." Can you spot six shooting stars in this picture?

Talking Tess takes a taxi

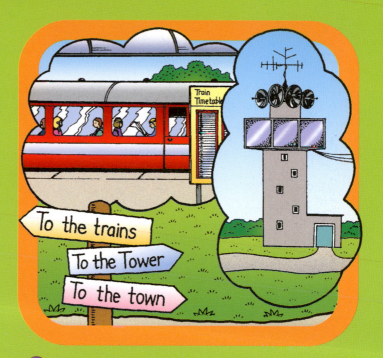

1 Talking Tess is waiting for a taxi.

2 Where will the taxi take her?

3 A taxi comes along and Tess gets in.

4 Tess looks out of the taxi window.

5 She sees ten trees and some toadstools...

6 ...and two tents and a teapot.

Town centre 2 miles

TELEPHONE

7 Then Talking Tess sees a tractor and a telephone box as she travels in a taxi to...

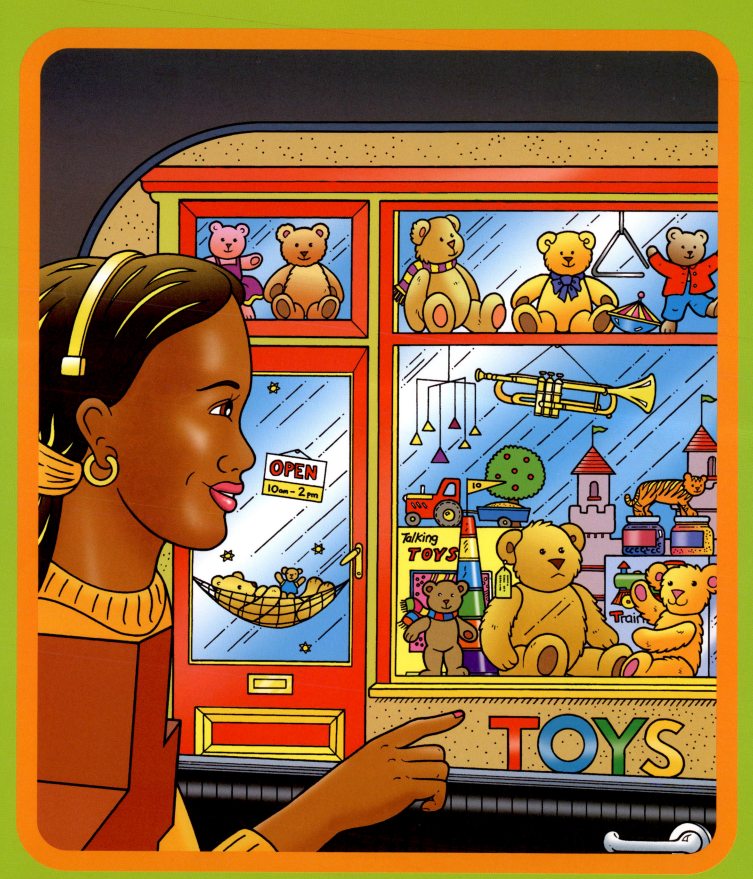

8 ...a terrific toyshop that's full of toys! How many teddy bears can you see in the window?

Uppy Umbrella gets upside down

1 Uppy Umbrella flies up, up and away.

2 She flies up under the trees.

3 She flies up to Lucy's lighthouse.

4 She flies upstairs and out of the window...

5 …and lands upside down…

6 …in a tree! Now Uppy is very upset!

7 "Oh dear, that's unlucky", says Lucy Lamp Light. "Poor Uppy Umbrella is stuck upside down in a tree."

8 But here comes Firefighter Fred. He will soon untangle her. How many umbrellas can you count in the tree?

Vicky and Walter team up

1 Vicky Violet is delivering vegetables.

2 Oh no! Her van has broken down.

3 "Don't worry," says Walter Walrus.

4 "We can use my wheelbarrow!"

5 "Thank you very much," says Vicky.

6 Soon Walter Walrus's wheelbarrow is full.

7 Vicky and Walter deliver the vegetables to the castle. "You're just in time," says Kicking King.

8 And he invites Vicky and Walter to join him for a delicious meal. Who is helping Kicking King in the kitchen?

Fix-it Max and Yo-yo Man stage

1 Zig Zag Zebra is running a race…

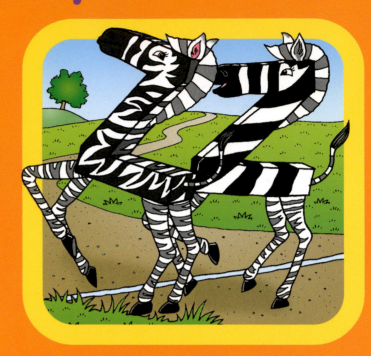

2 …against her best friend Zoe.

3 "Ready, steady, go!" yells Yellow Yo-yo Man.

4 Fix-it Max is excited to see the zebras run.

a Zebra Race

5 The zebras zoom up a steep hill...

6 ...and zoom all the way down again.

7 "Don't stop now!" Clever Cat and Harry Hat Man cheer. "You're nearly there!"

8 "Excellent!" cries Fix-it Max. "You both win!" yells Yellow Yo-yo Man. How many trophies is Fix-it Max holding?

Quarrelsome Queen's Questions

Look at the pictures, read the text, and see if you can answers these questions.

1 Where does Annie Apple live?

2 What kind of flowers does Bouncy Ben pick?

3 What type of cake does Clever Cat like best?

4 What does Dippy Duck draw for Clever Cat?

5 Eddy Elephant won the race, but who came in second?

6 Who does Firefighter Fred feed on the farm?

7 Where does Golden Girl find Bouncy Ben?

8 What's Harry Hat Man's horse called?

9 What type of insect does Impy Ink paint?

10 Why is Jumping Jim feeling so jolly?

11 Who paints Kicking King's kite?

12 Where does Lucy Lamp Light live?

13 What does Munching Mike make?

14 What is Noisy Nick reading?

15 Where does Oscar Orange fall asleep?

16 What kind of musical instrument does Peter Puppy like to play?

17 What does Quarrelsome Queen use to cover her bed?

18 Where does Red Robot get stuck?

19 What does Sammy Snake see through the telescope?

20 Where does Talking Tess go in her taxi?

21 Why does Uppy Umbrella get upset?

22 What kind of food does Vicky Violet like best?

23 What does Walter Walrus let Vicky Violet use?

24 Why does Fix-it Max get excited?

25 What does Yellow Yo-yo Man yell to start the race?

26 What is Zig Zag Zebra's best friend called?

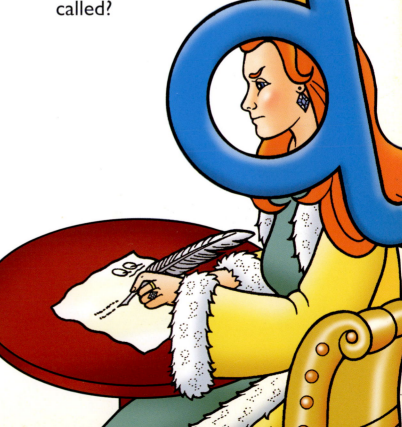

The Letterlanders

 Annie Apple

 **Bouncy Ben**

 **Clever Cat**

 **Dippy Duck**

 **Eddy Elephant**

 **Firefighter Fred**

 **Golden Girl**

 **Harry Hat Man**

 **Impy Ink**

 **Jumping Jim**

 **Kicking King**

 **Lucy Lamp Light**

 **Munching Mike**

 **Noisy Nick**

 Oscar Orange

 **Peter Puppy**

 **Quarrelsome Queen**

 **Red Robot**

 **Sammy Snake**

 **Talking Tess**

 **Uppy Umbrella**

 **Vicky Violet**

 **Walter Walrus**

 **Fix-it Max**

 **Yellow Yo-yo Man**

 **Zig Zag Zebra**

Letterland

ABC

Trusted by parents and teachers, loved by children

First reading flashcards

Age 3+

Second reading flashcards

Age 4+

Rhyming flashcards

Age 3+

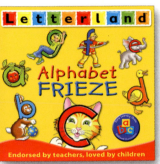

Alphabet FRIEZE

Endorsed by teachers, loved by children

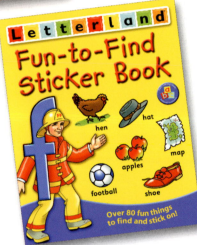

Fun-to-Find Sticker Book

hen · hat · map · apples · football · shoe

Over 80 fun things to find and stick on!

First Sticker Dictionary

car · cat · cake · dog · doll

40 fun stickers to help you learn the alphabet!

In the Jungle

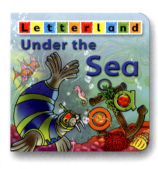

Under the Sea

On the Go!

At the Seaside

Action Songs

Sing the songs, do the actions and learn the alphabet

Alphabet Songs

NEW EDITION

26 lively songs to help teach your child letter sounds

Handwriting Songs

NEW EDITION

26 lively songs to help teach your child letter shapes

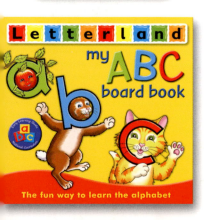

my ABC board book

The fun way to learn the alphabet

First Picture Word Book

plane · balloon · yacht · boat · sun ·

Trusted by parents and teachers, loved by children

Alphabet Adventures

Alphabet of Rhymes

For more information about Letterland products, log onto our website at
www.letterland.com   Or you can e-mail us at info@letterland.com

The end